ECHOES OF LAUGHTER: A TRIBUTE TO MY MOTHER'S JOYFUL LEGACY

FOND MEMORIES OF AAI (MY MOTHER), WHOM THE WORLD KNEW AS DR JAHAGIRDAR, WHO HAD GIFTED TO OVER 10,000 WOMEN, THE MOST PRECIOUS GIFT ANY WOMAN CAN EXPECT TO RECEIVE, MOTHERHOOD

DR. ASHOK JAHAGIRDAR PHD
(INFORMATION TECHNOLOGY)

Made with ♥ on the Notion Press Platform
www.notionpress.com

Contents

Preface

After my mother passed away after a unsuccessful surgery I realised that there were countless people who's lives she had touched so I thought that I would share memories I have of her. But I wanted these memories to make you smile or even burst out in laughter. Im sure she would have liked it that way

"In the tender tapestry of life, there are moments that etch themselves into the fabric of our existence, weaving together memories both poignant and profound. The passing of a loved one often serves as a catalyst for introspection, a reflective journey through the annals of shared experiences."

It is within this realm of remembrance, amidst the ebb and flow of emotions, that I find myself compelled to embark upon a voyage of storytelling.

The genesis of this endeavour traces back to a pivotal juncture arabsin my life, a moment steeped in sorrow yet illuminated by the radiant legacy of a remarkable woman. It was after my mother's untimely departure,

following an unsuccessful surgery, that I found solace in the luminous tapestry of her enduring influence. In the wake of her passing, I was enveloped by a profound realization: that the essence of her being transcended the confines of mortality, echoing through the lives of countless souls she had touched with her boundless love and unwavering compassion.

As I grappled with the depths of grief, an idea began to germinate—a fervent desire to immortalize the myriad moments of joy, laughter, and warmth that defined my relationship with her. Yet, I yearned for these recollections to transcend the somber veil of mourning, to evoke not only tears of nostalgia but also tears of mirth. For my mother, with her irrepressible spirit and infectious laughter, was a beacon of light in a world often shrouded in darkness. And so, I resolved to embark upon a literary odyssey — a tribute infused with the essence of her vivacity and zest for life.

Within the pages that follow, I invite you to traverse the landscape of my memories—a kaleidoscope of anecdotes and vignettes that paint a portrait of a woman whose laughter resonated like the chime of a bell. These are not merely tales of wistful reminiscence, but rather, windows into the soul of a woman whose love knew no bounds—a woman whose mere presence had the power to uplift spirits and ignite joy in the hearts of those fortunate enough to bask in her glow.

As I pen these words, I am acutely aware of the profound responsibility bestowed upon me—to capture the essence of my mother's essence with the reverence it deserves, while imbuing each narrative with the warmth and levity that defined her character. For she was more than a mere mortal; she was a force of nature, a wellspring of unconditional love and unwavering support — a beacon of hope in a world often fraught with uncertainty.

It is my fervent hope that within these pages, you will find solace, laughter, and perhaps even a glimpse of your own cherished memories mirrored in the reflections of my own. For in the act of sharing, we forge connections that transcend the boundaries of time and space, weaving together the disparate threads of our lives into a tapestry of shared humanity.

And so, I invite you to embark upon this journey with me — a journey illuminated by the radiant spirit of a woman whose memory will forever be enshrined in the collective consciousness of all who had the privilege of knowing her.

CHAPTER ONE

A Beacon in the Storm

Once late in the evening, when riots were tearing through the heart of the city, my mother, received a call from the hospital. A patient was in labour, and the urgency in the nurse's voice left no room for hesitation. Riots or not, it made no difference to my mother. She was a doctor, and a life was about to enter the world.

With determination etched on her face, she took the stethoscope in one hand the car keys in the other, and headed to the garage. The distant sound of chaos – shouts, breaking glass, the occasional wail of a siren – filled the air, but it did not deter her. She backed the car out and chose the route she thought was the safest, weaving through side streets and alleys, away from the main areas of unrest.

As she neared the hospital, she saw a throng of rioters up ahead, stones in hand, their faces contorted with anger and frustration. She slowed the car, her heart pounding, and took a deep breath. Putting her hand out of the window, she waved, hoping against hope that someone would listen.

A young man, barely older than a boy, approached the car, suspicion in his eyes. My mother leaned out and said calmly, "I am a doctor. There's a woman in labor at the hospital. I need to get there to deliver her baby."

The boy's expression softened, and he turned to the crowd behind him. "Stop! Doctor going to the hospital!" he shouted.

In an instant, the stone-throwing ceased. A path opened up, and the rioters stepped back, allowing her car to pass. She drove through the makeshift corridor they had created, her hands steady on the wheel, her mind focused on the task ahead.

Minutes later, she arrived at the hospital, where the staff greeted her with relieved smiles. She scrubbed in quickly and headed to the delivery room. The expectant mother was in distress, but the sight of my mother brought a measure of calm to the room.

Hours passed a blur of concentrated effort, and finally, a healthy cry filled the air. My mother held up a bonny baby, tears of joy streaming down the new parents' faces. It was a moment of pure, unadulterated life amidst the turmoil outside.

As she handed the baby to its mother, im sure Aai (as I affectionately called her) must have felt a deep sense of fulfillment. She knew that for every act of violence, there was also an act of kindness, for every tear of sorrow, a tear of joy. In that moment, she was not just a doctor; she was a beacon of hope, a symbol of resilience.

When she left the hospital, it was early morning. The streets were quiet, the riots having subsided with the night. As she drove home, she thought about the young rioter who had stopped the crowd for her. She realized that even in the midst of chaos, humanity could shine through.

And so, the story of that night became a cherished memory, a testament to the power of compassion and the unwavering duty of a doctor. Aai, had brought a new life into the world against all odds, proving that even in the darkest of times, there is always a glimmer of light.

CHAPTER TWO

Lessons of Resilience: A Mother's Wisdom

Turning 18 marks a significant milestone in one's journey through life. It's a time of celebration, of newfound freedoms, and of embarking upon the threshold of adulthood. Yet, amidst the joyous festivities, there are moments of profound wisdom that shape our perspective and guide us through the labyrinth of life.

For me, this pivotal moment occurred when my mother, amidst the jubilation of my 18th birthday, pulled me aside to impart a lesson that would resonate with me for decades to come. As she beckoned me to a quiet corner, her words carried the weight of experience and the depth of a mother's love. "Sit," she said gently, "there's something I want to tell you."

In that intimate moment, amidst the cacophony of celebration, my mother's voice cut through the noise, offering a nugget of timeless wisdom that transcends generations. "In life, when you fall, don't fail. Get up. And don't blame yourself when you fail. It may be because of reasons beyond your control."

Her words struck a chord deep within me, resonating with the uncertainties and challenges that lay ahead. In a world where failure is often stigmatized and self-blame becomes a default reaction, my mother's words served as a beacon of resilience and self-compassion.

As tears welled in my eyes, overwhelmed by the depth of her wisdom and the unconditional love she bestowed upon me, I reached out and touched her feet—a gesture of reverence and gratitude ingrained in our cultural heritage. "Thank you, Aai," I whispered, my voice choked with emotion.

We returned to the festivities, the echoes of her words reverberating in my mind. From that moment onward, her advice became my guiding principle—a compass to navigate the turbulent seas of life with grace and fortitude.

Now, at the age of 64, reflecting upon the journey that has unfolded since that fateful birthday, I realize that my mother's words have been a constant companion—a source of strength in moments of adversity, a reminder of resilience in the face of setbacks, and a beacon of hope in times of darkness.

Without a doubt, among all the gifts and well-wishes I have received over the years, my mother's words remain the most precious of all. For they are not merely words spoken in passing but a legacy of resilience and love—a timeless treasure that continues to illuminate my path, guiding me toward a life lived with purpose, perseverance, and compassion.

CHAPTER THREE

Humbling Encounter: Recognizing True Respect for a Senior Colleague

One evening, as the day was drawing to a close, a momentous encounter was about to unfold, at home, igniting a profound realization of respect and admiration. Dr. Pai Dhungat, a distinguished senior colleague of my mother had come to pay his respects to her. Though Dr. Pai himself was a father figure to the medical fraternity, he had not forgotten that my mother had welcomed him when he had first joined Bombay Hospital. I met him downstairs and we were entering the lift when Dr. Mrs. Vandana Phadke, the esteemed owner of one of the most reputable path labs, was passing by. She immediately came and in a gesture deeply rooted in tradition and reverence, she humbly touched Dr. Pai's feet.

However, what unfolded next was a testament to the intricate tapestry of professional respect and courtesy. Despite the unexpected reverence bestowed upon him, Dr.

Pai's demeanour remained unchanged, displaying an aura of humility and grace. In response to Dr. Phadke's introduction, he simply nodded his head, adorned with a warm smile, and inquired about her well-being.

Dr. Vandana Phudke, representing Phudke Labs, reciprocated the courteous exchange with equal poise and respect. "Very well, thank you, sir," she replied graciously before gracefully taking her leave. The interaction, though brief, encapsulated the essence of mutual admiration and professional courtesy.

Upon entering the familiar comfort of our home, a transformative moment unfolded. Dr. Pai's demeanor underwent a subtle yet profound shift as he laid eyes upon my mother. With a gesture that spoke volumes, he lowered his head and placed it at my mother's feet, a gesture of utmost reverence and respect.

In that poignant moment, a flood of realization washed over me like a gentle tide. It dawned on me with crystal clarity – the depth of respect and admiration that my mother commanded within her professional sphere. Dr. Pai's humble gesture served as a mirror, reflecting the profound impact of her contributions and the profound respect she had garnered over the years.

It was a revelation that transcended mere professional accolades; it was a testament to the indelible mark my mother had left on the hearts and minds of her colleagues. Through her unwavering dedication, expertise, and unwavering commitment to patient care, she had earned not only their admiration but their deepest respect.

In that fleeting yet profound moment, I witnessed the essence of true respect – not merely in words or gestures, but in the profound reverence that emanated from Dr. Pai's heartfelt gesture. It was a humbling reminder of the power of integrity, humility, and unwavering dedication in earning the respect of one's peers.

As I reflect on that transformative encounter, I am reminded of the profound impact that one individual can have on those around them. Through her exemplary leadership and unwavering commitment to her profession, my mother had earned the highest accolade – the genuine respect and admiration of her colleagues. And in that realization, I found solace, pride, and an unwavering sense of gratitude for the remarkable woman she was.

CHAPTER FOUR

Ticket Troubles: A Comedic Conundrum At Dadar Station

One of the memories that stands out, is as Aai as I called my mother and myself had gone to Dadar station to purchase railway tickets. The clerk at the counter asked my mother to fill up a form with the names of those travelling .There were only the 2 of us.

When he saw the 1st name Sharad he looked at me - I was about 7 years at that time - and asked"Are you Sharad?" My mother interrupted and said, "No I'm Sharad". He said "Ok, Sharada" and was about make the change on the form. Aai protested "No, not Sharada, Sharad." Sharad is usually almost always a mans name. He smiled weakly at aai and said "Madam Sharad is a man's name, your name must be Sharada". With the innocent audacity only a child possesses, I tugged at the pallu of her sari and asked her to show him her driving licence.

It clearly said there Dr Mrs Sharad Jahagirdar. Reluctantly he took the form and while handing over the tickets by he again weakly smiled and said ,"But it's unusual isnt it?" I could see a storm coming up..i dragged my mother away.

CHAPTER FIVE

Maternal Mastery: The Hidden Talents of a Table Tennis Champion

In the languid days of summer vacation, there was a ritualistic pilgrimage my family made to the tranquil haven of Club Mahableshwar. Amidst the verdant hills and cool breeze, nestled within the heart of the club, lay a sanctuary of recreation—the games room, where the rhythmic clack of table tennis paddles echoed through the air.

It was during one such sojourn that my mother, surprised me with an impromptu invitation to play. As she tucked her pallu aside, revealing a determination unbefitting of her graceful demeanor, I watched in awe as she confidently gripped the table tennis racket, scrutinizing its pimpled and non-pimpled sides with the scrutiny of a seasoned player.

Perplexed by her sudden enthusiasm, I stood ready, unknowing of the hidden depths of her skill. With a flick of her wrist, she requested the ball, and as I obliged, she began to bounce it on the table with the precision of a professional, gauging its speed with a practiced eye.

Then, with a nonchalant grace she motioned for me to serve. With trepidation, I sent the ball sailing towards her backhand, expecting a routine return. Yet, what transpired next defied all logic and expectation.

In a seamless motion, my mother executed a maneuver so swift and fluid, it seemed almost supernatural. Twisting her racket mid-swing, she transformed her backhand into a ferocious forehand smash, propelling the ball with an intensity that left me scrambling in disbelief.

Upon our return to Bombay, fueled by curiosity and admiration, I ventured to replicate her feat in my table tennis class. Yet, try as I might, I found myself ensnared in a web of fumbled attempts and lost balance, unable to grasp the elusive technique behind her skill.

It was then, in a moment of candid revelation, that my mother unveiled the secret of her mastery—a drawer nestled within her cupboard, housing the tangible evidence of her triumphs: two gleaming medals, testaments to her prowess as the intercollegiate women's singles and mixed doubles champion.

In that instant, enveloped in the warmth of her embrace, I realized that beneath the guise of maternal gentility lay a titan of talent, whose quiet achievements spoke volumes of her indomitable spirit and unwavering determination. And as I held her close, I knew that her legacy would forever inspire me to strive for greatness, both on and off the table.

CHAPTER SIX

Defying Conventions: The Courageous Journey of My Mother Behind The Wheel

In the annals of my memory, one particular anecdote stands out as a testament to the unwavering courage and determination of my mother—a narrative that transcends time, echoingY the resolute spirit of a woman who dared to defy societal norms and expectations.

During the tenure of my grandfather, whom I fondly called Ajoba, as a judge at the Bombay High Court, my mother harbored a silent aspiration—to learn how to drive. However, the barriers seemed insurmountable, as she was not of the age deemed appropriate for such pursuits. Undeterred by the constraints of convention, she embarked on a quiet rebellion, seeking to carve out her own path in a world defined by rigid gender roles and expectations.

In a moment of audacity, my mother approached the family driver, a figure of authority bound by allegiance to my grandfather. With a hushed tone that betrayed her resolve, she made her request known—to be taught the art of driving. Yet, the response she received was not one of encouragement but rather of apprehension. "Saheb will get angry with me," the driver murmured, his hesitation palpable in the air. Unfazed by the prospect of reprimand, my mother uttered words that would come to symbolize her defiance: "Don't worry, I'll handle that."

And so, under the cloak of secrecy and against the backdrop of disapproval, my mother embarked on her journey to mastery. The Ambassador car, a symbol of prestige and power, became her canvas, and the bustling streets of Bombay her proving ground. With a determination that knew no bounds, she navigated the intricacies of driving, defying expectations and societal norms with each turn of the wheel.

Years passed, and circumstances shifted, yet the memory of my mother's courageous endeavor remained etched in my mind—a beacon of inspiration in a world often marred by conformity and complacency. It was during our time in Nasik, a chapter in our family's narrative, that the impact of her defiance became manifest.

As my mother assumed her place behind the wheel, a group of schoolchildren passed by, their youthful curiosity piqued by the sight before them. In tones tinged with astonishment, they whispered amongst themselves, "See, see, there is a lady driving the car." In that moment, my mother transcended the confines of gender stereotypes, her actions serving as a reminder that courage knows no gender, no age, no limitations.

In conclusion, the journey of my mother behind the wheel is not merely a tale of learning to drive; it is a testament to the power of courage, determination, and defiance in the face of adversity. Through her actions, she challenged societal expectations, paving the way

With determination as her compass and courage as her guide, she navigated the complexities of driving with a grace that belied her age.

Years passed, and circumstances shifted, yet the memory of my mother's courageous endeavor remained a beacon of inspiration. It was during our time in Nasik, a moment frozen in the annals of memory, that the impact of her defiance became manifest.

As my mother assumed her place behind the wheel, a group of schoolchildren passed by, their youthful curiosity piqued by the sight before them. In tones tinged with astonishment, they whispered amongst themselves, "See, see, there is a lady driving the car." In that moment, my mother transcended the confines of gender stereotypes, challenging societal expectations, paving the way for future generations to embrace their dreams and aspirations with unwavering conviction. In her quiet rebellion, she embodied the essence of courage—the courage to defy, the courage to challenge, and the courage to chart one's own course in a world defined by boundaries and barriers.

CHAPTER SEVEN

Roots and Raindrops

In the heart of Satara, where monsoon clouds danced with the trees, a tale unfolded beneath the rain-soaked canopy of memories.

My mother had told me that though she had achieved success in the medical profession, she had not forgotten her roots,She had said to me " I had to wake up early so that I could finish my morning toilet activities behind the bushes so as not to be seen. often recalled these words as the rain cascaded down the windowpane, blurring the world outside.

It was one of those days when the rain seemed to embrace the town in a tight, wet hug, refusing to let go. As I stood by the roadside, watching the raindrops race each other down the glass, a familiar figure emerged from the mist – my mother.

She navigated through the downpour, her steps steady and purposeful, a testament to the resilience she had learned from her humble beginnings. I offered her shelter under my umbrella, and together we ventured through the downpour.

"Would you like to have some onion pakoda?" I asked, gesturing towards a humble cart nestled by the roadside. Despite the rain, the aroma of fried onions lingered in the air, tempting even the most reluctant palate.

"Sure," my mother replied with a smile, her eyes reflecting a hint of nostalgia. She parked the car and the rain eased into a gentle drizzle, as if granting us a moment of respite.

There was a particular cart, a familiar sight in the maze of vendors. As we approached, the seller's eyes lit up with recognition. "Namaste, Ashok bhai," he greeted, his voice warm and familiar.

He glanced at my mother, a silent question lingering in his gaze. I stepped forward, eager to introduce her. "This is my mother," I announced proudly, a sense of reverence coloring my words.

The seller nodded, understanding passing between them like an unspoken bond. With practiced efficiency, he cleaned a plastic stool and motioned for my mother to sit. She accepted the gesture with gratitude, her smile a reflection of the kindness she had encountered in every corner of her journey.

As the seller turned to me, I placed our order without hesitation. "The usual," I confirmed, a sense of familiarity settling over us like an old friend.

Within moments, he served my mother a steaming plate of onion pakodas, each morsel a testament to the flavors of home. She savored each bite, the taste transporting her back to a time when life was simpler, yet filled with its own brand of magic.

"How are they?" the seller inquired, his gaze shifting between us with genuine curiosity. My mother responded with a thumbs-up, her approval evident in the sparkle of her eyes.

Before we could protest, he produced a bottle of cold mango juice, a gesture of hospitality that transcended mere customer relations. My mother hesitated, her humility shining through even in the face of such generosity.

But the seller persisted, his words echoing with a sincerity that touched our hearts. "If you are Ashok bhai's mother, you are my mother too," he declared, his voice carrying the weight of a truth that resonated deep within us.

And in that moment, beneath the canopy of rain-soaked memories, we were reminded of the unbreakable bonds that connected us all – a reminder that no matter how far we journeyed, our roots would forever anchor us to the essence of who we were.

CHAPTER EIGHT

A Mother's Balancing Act

The year was 1966, and I was in the 2nd standard at the Malabar Hill infant school. Lunch time was a much-anticipated break in the day, a chance to run free for a little while and savour the midday meal.

We had the option of carrying our lunches or having them brought to us. My mother, despite her demanding career as a doctor at Bombay Hospital, insisted that I have a fresh, homemade lunch every day.

At that time, my mother's medical practice was thriving. She had trained under the illustrious Dr. V. N. Shirodkar, renowned for his pioneering Shirodkar loop procedure, which helped countless women conceive. My mother was his natural successor, embodying the same dedication and skill that had made him famous. Yet, despite her burgeoning career, her commitment to her profession was matched only by her devotion to me.

The lunch bell would ring, and my heart would leap with excitement. I would rush to the school gates, eagerly scanning the road for my mother's car. As soon as I spotted it, I would run out, my small legs pumping with anticipation. My mother would park, and then the magic would begin.

With a practiced grace, she would spread a newspaper on the car's bonnet, creating an impromptu dining table. She would uncover the dish she had brought, the aroma of fresh chapattis and vegetables wafting through the air. The food was always warm, a testament to her impeccable timing and the love she infused into every meal.

First, she would lay out the chapattis, soft and steaming. Then came the vegetables, a colorful assortment cooked to perfection. She would watch with a tender smile as I ate, savoring each bite. The climax of this daily ritual was the buttermilk, cool and refreshing, poured with care into a small tumbler.

Once I had finished, my mother would meticulously clean the dishes with water from a bottle, drying them with a napkin before packing everything back into the basket. She would give me a quick hug, her eyes filled with warmth, and then drive back to the hospital, ready to dive into her afternoon appointments.

To this day, I marvel at how she managed it all: performing surgeries in the morning, rushing home to prepare my lunch, delivering it to school, and then returning to her patients, often working late into the evening. Her days were a delicate balance of professional excellence and personal devotion, a testament to her remarkable strength and love.

Those lunches were more than just meals; they were a symbol of my mother's unwavering commitment to me. Each bite was a reminder of her love and dedication, a lesson in the art of balancing career and family with grace and precision. Even now, the memory of those lunches warms my heart and inspires me to strive for the same balance and devotion in my own life.

CHAPTER NINE

Hospital Drama Bow

I was standing at the main entrance of the MRC (Medical Research Center) building of Bombay Hospital with my mother by my side. Sharma Ji, the hospital aministrator, saw my mother, came over greeted her and then they were in conversation. Bombay Hospital was hosting an international conference.

My mother had launched her career here.

As a Japanese delegate strolled by. Sharma Ji called out to him, then pointed to my unsuspecting mother and says “She is the Maharani of the hospital”.

The delegate’s confusion was apparent. Sharmaji also sensed that. "Queen, Queen!" he said in a flash. Suddenly, it all clicked for the bewildered delegate.

With a graceful step back, the Japanese delegate bowed in my mom’s direction, treating her like royalty in the hallways of Bombay Hospital. And then he simply stood there. This time it was my mother who was confused. I whispered in her ear: "You’ve got to bow back!

And so, with hesitation she gave and slightly rigid bow. The Japanese delegate left beaming like he just won a game of Sudoku.

Epilogue

When my mother passed away after a lifetime of selfless service to her countless patients, my wife, Surela, and I knew that her legacy should not be forgotten. Her dedication, compassion, and unwavering commitment to her work left an indelible mark on all who knew her. We wanted to ensure that her spirit lived on in a meaningful way, inspiring future generations to embody the same values she held dear.

Bearing this in mind, we instituted an annual cash prize to be awarded to the student who stands first in the MD (Gynecology and Obstetrics) program. This prize is not merely a recognition of academic excellence but a tribute to the passion and dedication that my mother demonstrated throughout her career. It serves as a beacon of inspiration, encouraging young doctors to strive for excellence, compassion, and selflessness in their practice.

This prize is our way of ensuring that my mother's legacy endures for eternity, a perpetual reminder of her contributions to the field and her impact on countless lives. It is our hope that, through this prize, her spirit will continue to inspire and guide those who follow in her footsteps, fostering a new generation of doctors who are as committed to their patients as she was.

www.ingramcontent.com/pod-product-compliance
Lightning Source LLC
LaVergne TN
LVHW021203160826
845679LV00024B/2224

9798894751047